# CONTENTS

# WHERE HAVE WE BEEN?

# HIGH-TECH HIGHWAYS AND SUPER SKYWAYS

## THE NEXT 100 YEARS OF TRANSPORTATION

by Nikole Brooks Bethea

raintree

a Capstone company — publishers for children

Raintree is an imprint of Capstone Global Library Limited, a company incorporated in England and Wales having its registered office at 264 Banbury Road, Oxford, OX2 7DY Registered company number: 6695582

www.raintree.co.uk
myorders@raintree.co.uk

Edited by Mandy Robbins
Art Directed by Nathan Gassman
Designed by Ted Williams
Original illustrations © Capstone Global Library Limited 2017
Illustrated by Alan Brown
Coloured by Giovanni Pota
Picture research by Jo Miller
Production by Katy LaVigne
Originated by Capstone Press
Printed and bound in China

ISBN 978 1 4747 1214 9
20 19 18 17 16
10 9 8 7 6 5 4 3 2 1

British Library Cataloguing in Publication Data
A full catalogue record for this book is available from the British Library.

Acknowledgements
We would like to thank the following for permission to reproduce photographs: Design Element: Shutterstock: pixelparticle (backgrounds)

Every effort has been made to contact copyright holders of any material reproduced in this book. Any omissions will be rectified in subsequent printings if notice is given to the publisher.

Owning cars let people move out of the cities. They no longer had to live close to railway stations.

The convenience of automobiles gave people new freedoms. They travelled when and where they wanted.

Cars changed a lot from the Model T Ford in the 1950s and 1960s.

That's nothing compared to cars today. My mum's just bought a hybrid. It combines gas and electric power.

We are always improving technology. Cars have become faster, safer and smarter. But to discover even faster travel, let's check out air transportation.

# STREETCARS

All forms of transportation evolve over time. Consider the streetcar. In 1832 the first streetcars were pulled along steel rails by horses in New York, USA. By the 1870s, steam engine-powered cable cars began replacing horse-drawn streetcars. Moving cables between the tracks hauled these people-movers continuously down the streets. In the late 1880s, streetcars powered by electric overhead wires began to replace cable cars. But this technology soon gave way to subways, buses and other forms of public transportation in the 1900s.

The air exhibit includes early planes and full-size replicas of famous planes.

Wow!

Cool!

The Wright brothers' 1903 Flyer was the first powered aeroplane.

Their first flight lasted only 12 seconds, but it proved that air travel was a real possibility.

By 1918 air travel started improving our mail service with the development of airmail. These types of early planes were used by airmail service.

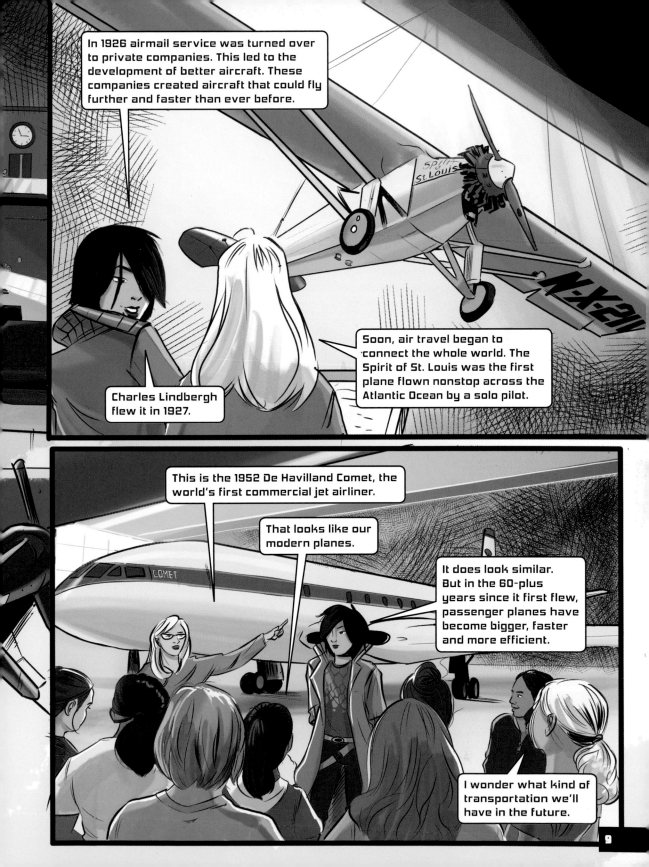

**WHERE ARE WE GOING NEXT?**

It's a gadget I invented. I can input data about choices people could make in the future. Then a hologram of what the future may look like pops up.

Whoa!

What's that?

Cool!

We know cars are getting smarter and smarter. But will there ever be self-driving cars?

Actually, companies such as Google are already looking into that possibility.

I can't wait to see how self-driving cars might operate.

Excuse me, sir. What did you type in?

My company's address. Now I can eat breakfast and catch up on the daily news on the way to work.

How does the car know where to go?

It uses lasers, radar and cameras to read road signs and traffic signals.

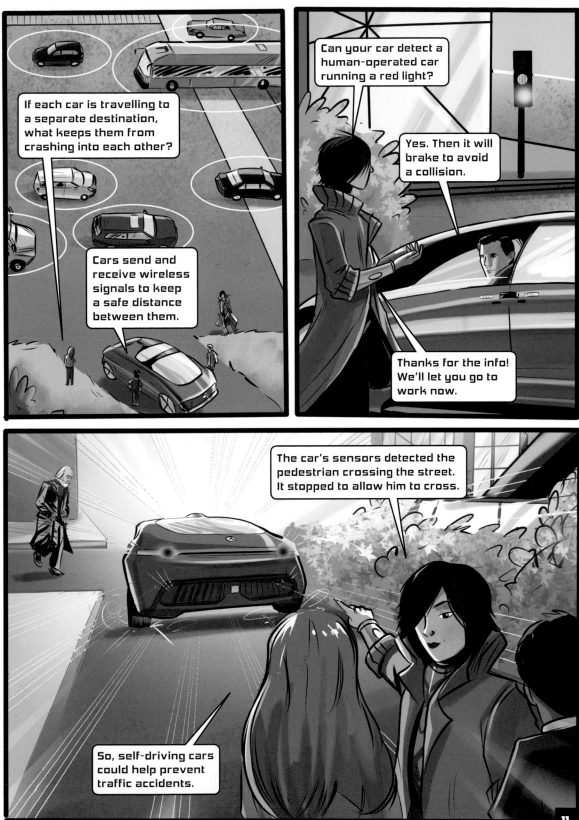

If cars will be able to drive themselves, will planes fly without pilots?

My dad says the military already has systems that can land a plane on an aircraft carrier.

It looks like we're about to find out!

Please take a seat. Fasten your seat belts. We'll be taking off soon.

So far, this seems like a normal flight.

So, how is this plane operated?

It is pilotless. The plane's controls must detect its position, guide it to its destination and determine changing wind speeds and direction.

Awesome! We're flying in a robot!

Will passenger jets ever travel faster than the speed of sound — like military jets do today?

Believe it or not, it's been done before. The Concorde was a supersonic passenger jet that last flew in 2003. But it was too loud to keep using.

Those planes look really cool!

Hi. I pilot this plane. Do you want to know more about it?

We want to learn about supersonic flight.

Supersonic flights travel faster than the speed of sound. That's faster than 1,225 kilometres per hour.

When an aircraft travels at the speed of sound, it creates a sonic boom.

That's a thunder-like sound caused by shock waves created when travelling that fast.

Supersonic flights over land were once banned because of their sonic boom. That upside-down V on the tail changes the airflow over the plane. It makes the boom quieter.

Not all of these planes have the upside-down V. Are they supersonic?

Yes. Other companies engineered the jets differently to make the sonic boom quieter.

All the supersonic designs have the same goal—cutting travel time.

The Concorde could fly from London to New York City in less than 3.5 hours. That's half the time of a regular aeroplane.

People always want to move faster and faster!

## HYPERLOOP

The Hyperloop is a proposed high-speed transportation system in California, USA. Capsules may one day transport passengers through a large tube from Los Angeles to San Francisco. The 563-kilometre (350-mile) trip is predicted to take about half an hour. The capsules would travel on a cushion of air through the tube at 1,223 kilometres (760 miles) per hour.

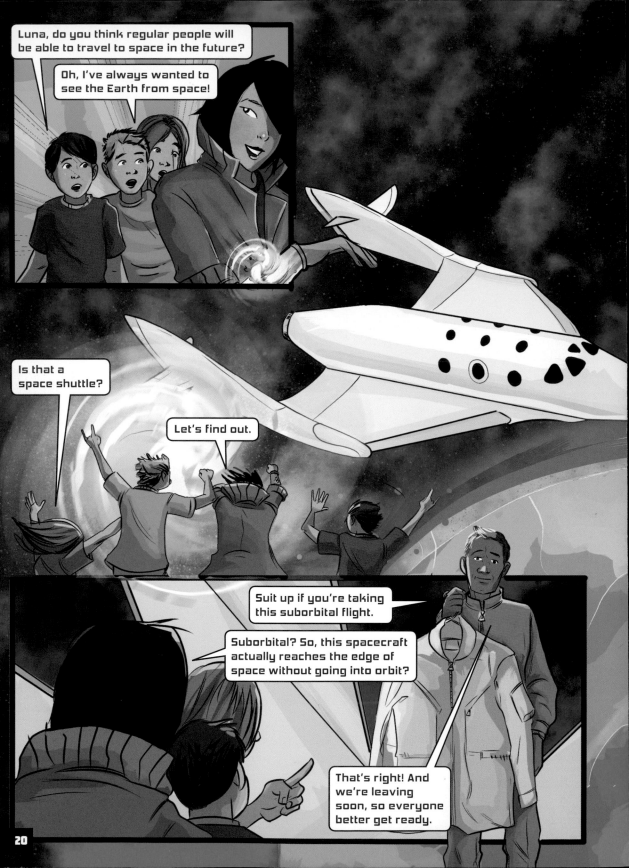

# BY THE YEAR 2120

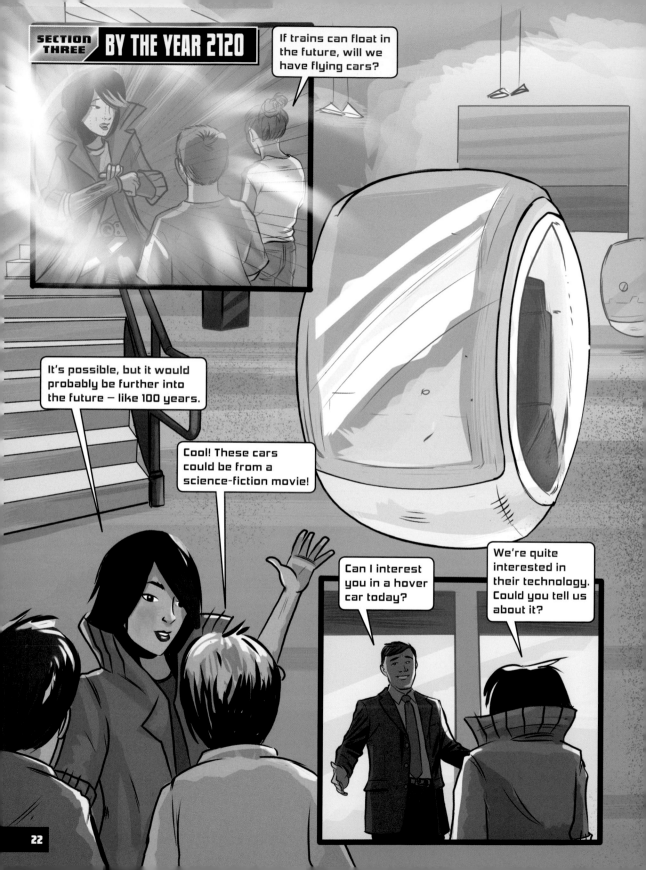

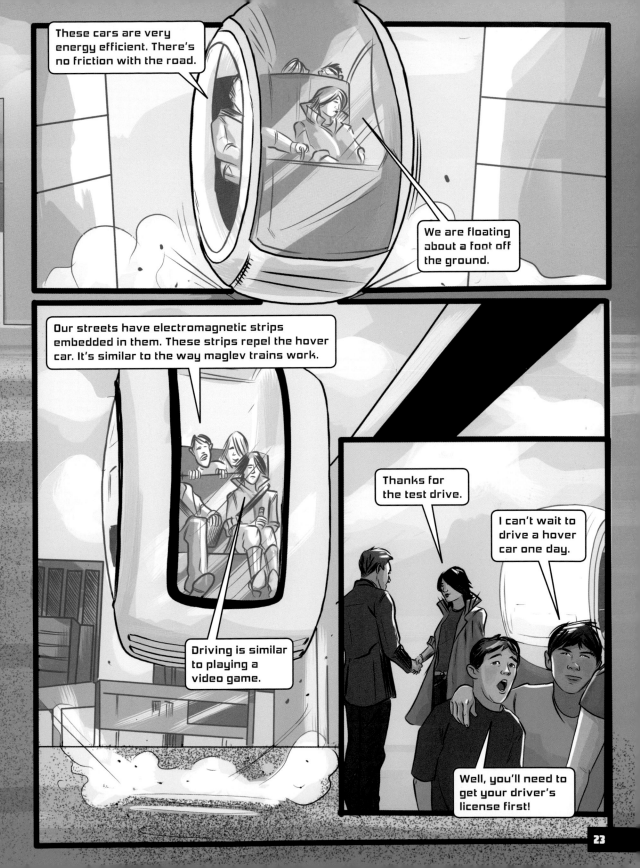

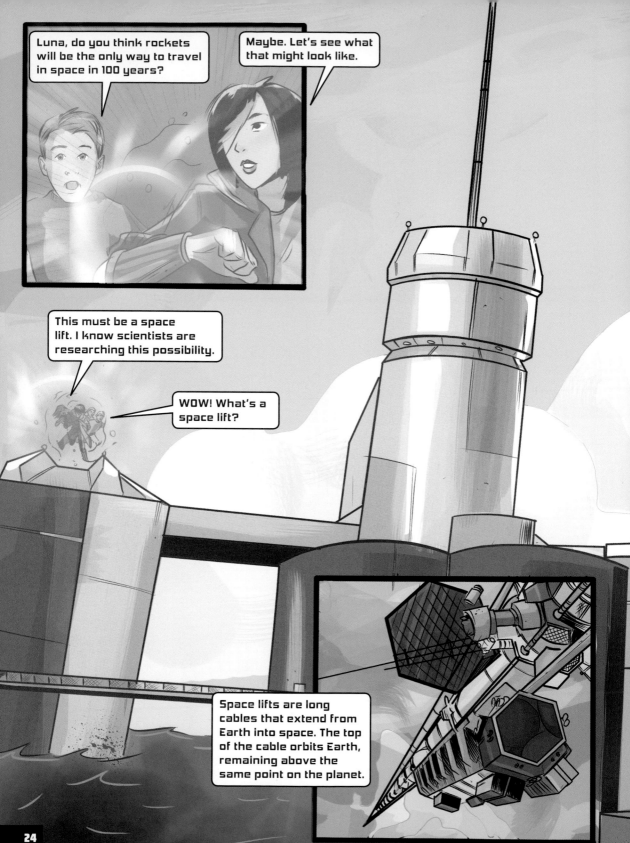

Luna, do you think rockets will be the only way to travel in space in 100 years?

Maybe. Let's see what that might look like.

This must be a space lift. I know scientists are researching this possibility.

WOW! What's a space lift?

Space lifts are long cables that extend from Earth into space. The top of the cable orbits Earth, remaining above the same point on the planet.

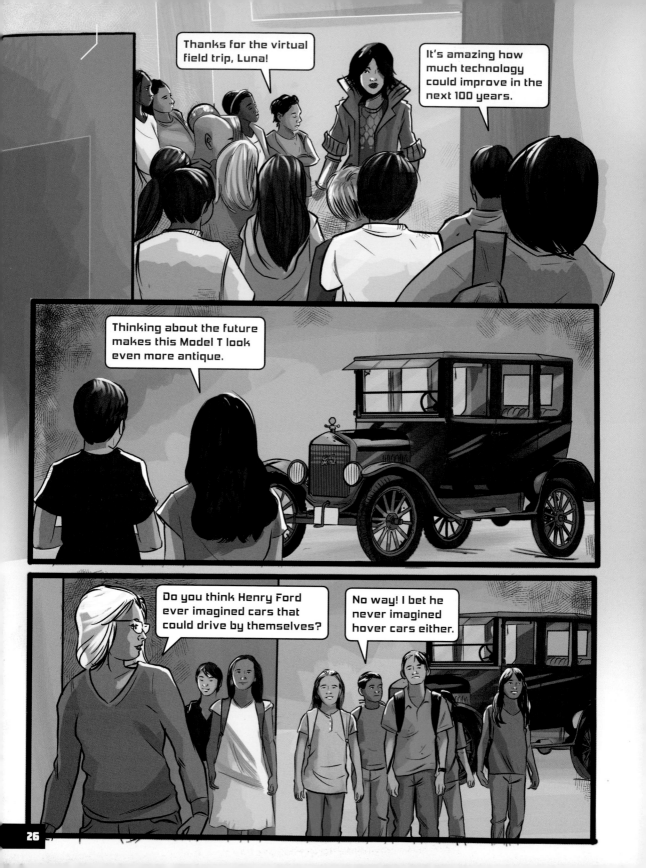

# TELEPORTATION

Today some scientists are looking into the possibility of teleportation that instantly transports an object from one place to another. Teleporting people is far beyond the abilities of today's scientists, but it could be possible in the distant future. In 2014 scientists in the Netherlands teleported subatomic particles from one point to another, 3 metres (3.3 yards) apart. Perhaps hundreds of years from now, scientists will figure out how to teleport goods or even people.

# TRANSPORTATION

Orville and Wilbur Wright's first powered aeroplane flight lasted only 12 seconds. It flew at Kitty Hawk, North Carolina, USA, on December 17, 1903. The flight distance was 36 metres (120 feet).

James Watt designed the steam engine in 1769 in Scotland. In 1825 George Stephenson designed the world's first railway locomotive in England for Stockton and Darlington Railway.

The Clermont was the first successful steamboat, built by Robert Fulton in 1807. Most steamboats built in the 1800s and 1900s had paddle wheels.

George Stevenson is considered to be the father of railways. In 1814 he built the first locomotive for commercial use.

Hydrogen may be a commonly used fuel for future transportation. The government estimates that by 2020, the United Kingdom will have 65 hydrogen filling stations. In 2015, there were 4 stations open for public use.

The Federal Aviation Administration (FAA) has given Amazon permission to research and test drone delivery in the United States. Amazon is restricted to testing no higher than 122 metres (400 feet) and no faster than 161 kilometres (100 miles) per hour. The drones must remain within sight of the operator. Additionally, drones must fly over private property.

LiftPort, a company in the United States, is currently researching the possibility of building a space elevator on the Moon. It could be used to transport building materials, supplies and people to a possible future colony on the Moon.

Alternative fuels are a growing trend in motor vehicles. Battery-operated vehicles such as the three-wheeled Arcimoto SRK may be the way of the future. The Arcimoto can travel up to 209 kilometres (130 miles) on a single charge of its battery pack.

## MORE ABOUT LUNA LI

Futurists are scientists who systematically study and explore possibilities about the future of human society and life on Earth. Luna proved herself to be brilliant in this field at a young age. She excelled in STEM subjects and earned her PhD in Alternative Futures from the University of Hawaii at Manoa. Luna invented a gadget she calls the Future Scenario Generator (FSG) that she wears on her wrist. Luna inputs current and predicted data into the FSG. It then crunches the numbers and creates a portal to a holographic reality that humans can enter and interact with.

# GLOSSARY

**electromagnet** temporary magnet created when an electric current flows through a conductor

**evolve** when something develops over a long time with gradual changes

**fossil fuels** natural fuels formed from the remains of plants and animals; coal, oil and natural gas are fossil fuels

**friction** force created when two objects rub together; friction slows down objects

**hypersonic** speed faster than Mach 5.0

**laser** narrow, intense beam of light

**orbit** path of one body around another

**radar** device that uses radio waves to track the location of objects

**replica** exact copy of something

**subatomic** describes things that are smaller than and part of an atom

**suborbital flight** flight into space that is too slow to orbit Earth

**supersonic** faster than the speed of sound

*Find Your Future in Engineering* (Bright Futures Press: Find Your Future in STEAM) Diane Lindsey Reeves (Cherry Lake Publishing, 2016)

*Future Explorers: Robots in Space* (Exploring Space and Beyond) Dr. Steve Kortenkamp (Capstone Press, 2015)

*Futureworld* (Tomorrow's Technology Today) Joel Levy (Carlton Books, 2014)

## WEBSITES

**http://www.bbc.com/future/story/20131108-what-will-we-be-driving-in-2050**
Learn about the cars we'll drive in 2050.

**http://www.sciencefocus.com/feature/future/future-technology-22-ideas-about-change-our-world**
Find out which ideas are going to change the world!